Pop Smoke
or the
Colonel in the
Helicopter

WILLIAM D. ROSE

PAGE PUBLISHING
Conneaut Lake, PA

First originally published by Page Publishing 2024

ISBN 979-8-89315-009-4 (pbk)
ISBN 979-8-89315-011-7 (digital)

Printed in the United States of America

Contents

Foreword

I suppose many of us who served in Vietnam thought we would write a book about our experiences in that conflict. Certainly, I felt that way while serving as a rifle platoon leader with the 199th Light Infantry Brigade from 1969 to 1970. (Additional information on the 199th's role in the war may be found in the index.) It's only taken me fifty-plus years to finally do it. This book is meant to offer insights derived from combat situations blended with experiences from a t hirty-five-year career in business with several building materials industry-segment leading US companies.

The episodes or anecdotes aren't meant to have deep meanings. In fact, I intend for these writings to offer simple advice that may prove useful to those who are beginning work careers or those who may be frustrated by events ongoing in their work's journey. Mostly, though, it is my desire to share the experiences of trying to lead and survive during my months on the ground in Vietnam.

Multitudes of self-help, business counsel books have been written over the years. I have read a number of them and gained some helpful ideas for my own work and life. One of the best is Dean Smith's *The Carolina Way*, which follows a format very similar to what this volume uses. I highly recommend it. I've also thought that my experiences could provide guidance that was at least entertaining and a way to keep Vietnam War lessons learned pertinent.

As with any input from a self-styled expert, take it for what it's worth. The events described are as accurate as my memory will allow. There is no intention to belittle or denigrate individuals who played various roles in Vietnam or afterward. Rather, each short episode/ chapter is designed to present, as we used to say, some "after-action lessons learned." While I have attempted to provide information in a somewhat rational chronological order, that may not always appear to be achieved.

The business situations that I found as parallels to military incidents are brief and as succinct as possible because any reader working in similar positions can adapt the lessons learned as applicable to his or her situation. The point is that even as times and people change, some basic tenets should always be in play. Achievement of the mission and welfare of the troops/employees must be appropriately balanced.

As evidence will show, I am certainly no polished, professional author. But my recollections and advice are as honest and forthright as I can make them, so candor may possibly make up for a lack of talent.

I hope the rambling and musings will be helpful and enjoyable to readers of the book.

Pop Smoke or the Colonel
in the Helicopter

During the course of my business career, it came to seem that financial types, more often than not, drove companies' actions, and sometimes, this kind of focus is very beneficial.

However, I have also come to believe that actions are what produce numbers (financial results). Many of the accountant types seem to think numbers produce results. Certainly, financial reports are good metrics. They help with goal setting and in determining how we perform against objectives. But to think that numbers analysis makes things happen is just not right. One of my colleagues used to say about one executive that "He's like the coach who runs the team by looking at the scoreboard, not what's happening on the field." Good results must ultimately be achieved or an organization fails (i.e., provides no value to stakeholders). Its participants, however, will perform because of good leadership, not because someone keeps flogging numbers and constantly reviewing them with operators.

This particular chapter is the source of my book's title. It's derived from truly frustrating Vietnam experiences with high-ranking officers—usually colonels—who insisted upon progress reports. Here's the story: Platoons in the 199th operated independently for the most part—separated from other platoons by over a kilometer in thick jungle. Movement in "triple canopy" jungle while attempting stealthy progress was not easy. It is difficult to follow the correct compass direction and to keep men in file yet properly spaced for security/safety and tactical purposes.

Now, at times, the battalion commander would orbit above our AO (area of operations) at a couple thousand feet in a helicopter and request progress reports by ordering units to "pop smoke!" (detonate a colored smoke grenade). This meant he wanted to see how far we had moved along our daily prescribed route of march, and the smoke rising from the jungle would denote our position. The maddening part—or parts—was that the progress never seemed to be acceptable to the colonel who had no clue regarding the difficulty of the terrain and that we were routinely divulging our position to any enemy in the area.

The mission was to seek, engage, and defeat the VC or NVA, but the emphasis seemed to be changed to simply "making numbers" or progress to satisfy the guy riding a chopper in much cooler, comfortable conditions with no idea of the situation on the ground.

Lesson learned: Organizations are run by human beings. Numbers are helpful guides and measures. They can help with modeling and planning. But when figures and statistics begin to outweigh common sense and smart and innovative ideas, then trouble can arise. People may start to fudge things to "make numbers." Certainly, reviewing progress can be useful in adjusting tactics or plans, but reports shouldn't be required to simply produce superfluous information.

How to Pack a Rucksack or
Let a Buddy Help You

Army training during the Vietnam era was like military training has always been: good and bad, thorough in places and insufficient in others, nasty and tedious. We were taught how to march, fire weapons, understand tactics (to a degree), and, ostensibly, how to lead. But there were always small details that get overlooked yet are important at field execution level.

Since the 199th's SOP (standard operating procedure) was to perform patrols lasting anywhere from three to twelve days, it was necessary to "pack" in quite a bit of gear: C rations, ammunition, grenades, water, poncho and poncho liner, claymore mines, some extra clothing such as socks, and a few personal hygiene items. One's rucksack had only limited storage capacity for these things, and one had only limited physical ability to carry over forty to fifty pounds of gear in the heat and humidity and difficult jungle terrain.

Infantry Officer Candidate School (OCS) provided some experience, but it was all for training—not the real thing. So after being issued a standard US Army rucksack upon arrival in Vietnam, I needed to pack it for my first mission with Second Platoon, A Company, Fifth Battalion, Twelfth Infantry, 199th Infantry Brigade, Light (SEP). Fortunately, another platoon leader who had more time in- country offered his advice of how to best pack a rucksack for easy and quick access to items and inclusion of really pertinent supplies. Without the benefit of Lt. Dave Weimer's actual field experience, I would've made a mess of my packing attempt. He assisted patiently and with explanations for why he chose to "pack a sack" as he guided me through the process.

Over time, I came to change some things to better suit my needs. But without initial help, I would've struggled during early patrols.

Lesson learned: New associates need help from experienced employees about how to do things efficiently and effectively. They should be paired with "A" players who will mentor them and instill good company and personal habits early on. Some senior associates seem to wait and watch while the rookie screws up and then offer advice. While learning from mistakes can be beneficial at times, a concerned partner helps build loyalty and promotes a future of service from the one he aided. Make sure your business understands the concept.

Four-Day Patrol or Wait—Stay Longer—Don't Mislead

I think people in general and Americans particularly hate to feel they've been misled. We do not want leaders to tell us what they think we want to hear. Knowing the reality is something else.

In Vietnam, our standard operating procedures on tactics within Fifth Battalion, Twelfth Infantry of the 199th Brigade were to perform patrols for three to four days, return to the fire support base for a couple of days to rest and resupply, and then go out again on another patrol. We basically went out on patrol every week.

In practice, however, after we had been on a mission for three days—using up the water and rations we had packed with us—and awaited orders for helicopter extraction or march-out orders, the platoon leader would get a message that we'd receive a resupply bird so we could continue reconning and setting ambushes. This was usually due to supposed new intelligence that enemy activity was reportedly expected, and we were ordered to move to a new location.

Well, sometimes, this situation could occur three or four times after the original mission began. My longest period of patrolling was fourteen days.

The point is don't give false expectations to the troops. You lose their trust, and morale declines. Tell it like it is to begin with: "Your platoon is being sent out for an initial three- or four-day mission and could be extended depending on enemy activity and the need for your further participation." Even though you may grow to understand this could happen, candor up front is appreciated.

When there's a negative situation, people will cling to potentially positive data. If it proves invalid, there's a big downside in attitude. Alternatively, when there is a surprise good news (e.g., being pulled out early), positive feelings arise.

Lesson learned: Be truthful with associates. Obviously, things can change, and actions must adjust accordingly for mission achievement. Big problems arise when things always seem to warrant changes, and leaders can lose credibility. After a while, plans and leaders aren't trusted when they aren't considered reliable.

Employees mustn't feel like they are simple pawns or "assets" without feelings. They see through disingenuous actions, and this eventually shows in their performance. Certainly, strategic plans can change—and may really need to minimize loss or adjust to competitive situations. But if they change too often, then it may mean the planners need changing.

Snake Bite Medevac or Unnecessary Risk

The first helicopter medevac or DUSTOFF that I was required to call in for my platoon was unusual, to say the least. Second platoon had been ordered to patrol from Firebase Libby and to set up day and night ambushes in a section of the battalion area of operations. It was relatively early in my stint as platoon leader, and I relied on the guys who were more experienced for advice and input since I was still learning. But I ultimately had to make decisions.

Our platoon had set up our nighttime ambush position in a dense jungle not near any well-traveled enemy trails. We didn't come across any signs that day. That night was dark as pitch, and I was told that two men in one of our five positions had been bitten by a snake.

Well, there were certainly a lot of snakes in the Vietnam jungles. Bamboo vipers were particularly dangerous. I got our medic, whom we all called Doc, to check the guys out. I did as well, trying to maintain light and noise discipline as we examined the men using a flashlight while covered with a poncho. One man was African American, and it was difficult to see fang marks. The other guy was White, and it appeared something had bitten him. But was it a snake?

There were numerous poisonous snakes in the country with the bamboo viper being one we really tried to avoid. I asked Doc if they were suffering from a snake bite. He said, "Could be."

They thought they were even though they hadn't identified a snake. Maybe a spider? Didn't know.

Well, if it was a poisonous snake bite and they didn't get treatment, it could mean death.

But, if it wasn't from a snake and I called for a DUSTOFF, it meant endangering pilots and crew and divulging our position. And it was at night.

I decided I could not take the risk of keeping the men out and would err on the side of caution. I radioed for the DUSTOFF.

Response was pretty quick, and the Huey was en route to us. However, it was so dark the pilot could not find our location even with me holding up a strobe light nestled in my helmet to keep the light from flashing all around our position.

As we tried to guide the chopper in, our battalion commander was listening back at the tactical operations center. He had the bright idea to fire an artillery, marking round over the map grid point, which I reported as our location.

A marking round explodes in midair and is designed to aid ground units prior to calling for the real, high-explosive shells to follow. If it's too close, the platoon leader can tell the battery to adjust its range before firing for effect.

As the helicopter continued to circle in the distance, the marking round came over and exploded *way* too near the chopper. It wasn't far from a direct hit. We could see the flash reflect off the bird's canopy.

The pilot very calmly said, "Check fire on the marking rounds. I'll have to circle around to get my night vision back."

Damn. Close call. It did allow us to know how near the DUSTOFF was, and we could guide it in. The colonel remained quiet at this point.

Of course, we then had to get the bitten men onto the chopper, and this required a jungle penetrator being lowered down through the trees as the bird hovered above. We accomplished the extraction, and the men received medical treatment.

Turned out, they were not bitten by a poisonous snake.

This episode exhibited command decisions can be very difficult and present potentially dangerous consequences. Welfare of the troops is very important while the achievement of the mission is paramount.

Our position was exposed; a medevac crew was put at risk and almost hit by friendly fire. Again, we were very lucky.

Lesson learned: The welfare of associates must be considered with great care. Get input and weigh potential consequences. Always try to minimize risk but realize there are a number of variables that may cause your mission to be compromised. Sometimes, individuals may overreact due to too much self-concern, and sometimes, well-meaning folks may cause negative issues. In the end, make a decision that is optimal.

Tabasco Sauce or Little Tricks of the Trade

There are a number of ways I test the authenticity of a VN vet's field experience. For those of us in the 199th, one of the small things was how we prepared those wonderful C ration meals when on patrol. C rations are not gourmet cuisine—much different from today's "meals ready to eat" (MREs) or even their forerunner, LRPs, as we called them, freeze-dried meals that were a treat when we got them. So I ask guys if they carried Tabasco sauce for their Cs. If they gave a blank stare, I know they may not have spent a lot of time in the boonies or lacked innovative C ration prep skills.

My introduction to Tabasco came on my first mission when my radio operator (RTO), Specialist Fourth Class Dick Tritt, advised me that a bit of Tabasco could sure spice up the otherwise bland C ration meal. He and other men on the platoon showed me how innovative they could be with C rations and a little Tabasco.

Businesses have their versions of Tabasco and how some mundane daily chores can be "spiced up." Rank-and-file associates learn about spicing—innovating. They like to share their ideas too, for the most part.

Lesson learned: Understand that the "regular folks" can be very inventive. They know some helpful things that you don't. Let them "spice up" your business with little tweaks that you've never thought about. Managers who focus mostly on the big picture can miss some very tasty (profitable) small ideas, and associates appreciate the opportunity to contribute.

Go Out on Patrol or Visit the Field

It's easy to stay back in a firebase (read: headquarters) where there are all types of comforts and services. While many liked to say there were no defined battle lines in Vietnam, it was certainly safer in a large rear base area such as Long Binh where the 199th's Brigade Main Base (BMB) was located. Occasional rocket attacks could and did occur, and during the Tet Offensive in 1968, a quite large battle was fought there.

However, patrols in the jungle with an undermanned platoon were definitely more difficult and dangerous. But if the enemy was to be found and eliminated, or at least his activities disrupted, then it was necessary to seek him out. And this meant getting onto his turf. The NVA or VC were masters at using the terrain of VN to their advantage. They knew the land and were used to hardships. Their tactics could negate the superior firepower of US forces.

As the war ground on, Americans learned to fight effectively in this environment, and the 199th's tactics kept the enemy at bay and reduced his relevance in our area of operations (AO). But only regular, aggressive patrols could maintain this condition.

(Note: Reference the terrible battering US Marines took at Khe Sanh. They essentially hunkered down in the outpost. Even if the strategy was to try and draw the NVA into a large, potentially decisive battle, you cannot just wait around to be attacked and decimated.)

Active patrolling meant knowing where the enemy was and what they were doing regarding base camps and movement. It meant a sharper, more skilled (albeit jumpy) group of US soldiers. It meant acquiring more respect for an enemy after understanding his situational tactics, thus not underestimating his capabilities.

Few folks enjoy deprivation and danger, but the experience defines one's outlook and confidence in achieving difficult goals.

Lesson learned: Business leaders must "go out in the field" and visit local company operations and customers on a regular basis. It gives a firsthand look and feel for situations facing a business. It shows you care, and it gets you away from "Yes Men" and a cocoon of comfort that belies what real value adders (or detractors) are doing. Local visits shouldn't be perfunctory and phony. They must be done with a genuine interest in what workers are doing in an often-difficult environment.

Likewise, customer visits should not be just a glad hand golf outing or fancy dinner. Rather, they should allow for valid intelligence gathering and showing true concern for the customer's enterprise. Make sure you go on patrol personally and regularly and with an agenda.

Jack at Your Back or
Share Information with the Troops

A rifle platoon is composed of a variety of individuals. Each man has a unique personality but also shares a number of common traits with others. For instance, some are pretty much scared to death all the time while others seem basically unaffected. Some seem smart, some not so smart. Some are willing to take orders, and others may dispute or dislike almost any command.

And some are simply curious. That was Jack's characteristic in my platoon in 1969. He seemed a bit more mature than some of the guys—maybe because he was over twenty years old, unlike so many.

As the person responsible for plotting our course as we moved on patrol through the jungle, I would stop periodically to check my map and take a compass reading. My platoon sergeant and I were the only individuals who were issued maps of the particular area of operations. While we conferred, the men could take a brief break and, after setting up in an appropriately secure manner, rest from humping a fifty-pound rucksack in 90 percent plus humidity.

Almost from the outset of assuming command, I began to notice that during these breaks, Jack would be hovering nearby as the platoon sergeant and I compared opinions on our progress and position. I felt his presence and perceived I was being watched or judged. Finally, one day, I asked the sergeant what Jack's deal was, and he answered, "Oh, Jack thinks he knows where we are or he wants to know where we are."

I thought, *Well, let's see what he thinks—maybe he does have some insights about things we've missed.*

So I invited Jack to look at the map and tell me what he thought. Did he notice any particular terrain features that the map showed? Did he agree with our pace count? We assigned an individual to count the paces (i.e., number of steps taken as we moved so we could estimate the distance traveled). Jack always had his ideas, and sometimes, they added to our own. But basically, I found that Jack simply felt more comfortable—perhaps safer—in being allowed to see the map and to participate in the discussion. And after several chances to participate, Jack became less interested and ceased to "hover."

Lesson learned: Now how does this story relate to the business world? There are a lot of "Jacks and Jills" in our organizations. They believe they know "where we should be going" or want to know where we are. They feel much more a part of the team—and much less fearful—when they are involved. Share the information. Ask for their opinions. You may be surprised—sometimes ol' Jack or Jill may have noticed something you missed entirely and help you get back on track. And while you can't involve every associate in all issues, you can build more trust and collaboration by sharing information appropriately.

Bring your people into the loop—share information that can be shared and ask for input. This shows recognition and creates more comfort and unity in the team.

Smart business leaders know associates from all levels of the organization have valuable insights. Allowing their ideas to be heard creates a positive ownership effect. Certainly, some ideas are self-serving and are meant to ease tasks. But mutual trust can result with the right amount of sharing.

War Trophy or Stand Up for Your People

My first week of patrolling with A Company involved multiple enemy contacts. Second Platoon was assigned to move with our company commander (CO) so he could observe my capabilities as the new guy and offer closer supervision. The CO liked operating in a cultivated area, designated AO Wichita as a company element, and sending a squad or platoon out as a separate nighttime ambush unit.

One night, I was ordered to take a squad out for an ambush when the main element positioned with the CO tripped claymore mines on a VC unit moving past their position. One of the men from my platoon triggered the mine, which wounded several enemies, including a VC medical officer who was carrying a 9-mm Browning Hi-Power pistol as a sidearm. This was an unusual event—a rare war trophy, which, by our standard operating procedures (SOP), was supposed to go to the soldier who caused the casualty or capture.

My squad was called back by the captain and managed to stumble our way to the company position where the wounded/captured enemy were medevaced, and we called in more close air support including Spooky—the old C-47 plane converted to a gunship with miniguns. It was a sight to see the stream of tracers fired where we thought the enemy had moved.

Sometime later, after we returned to our firebase and heard more about the after-action report for the contact, I learned our CO planned to keep the pistol we'd captured. This was not right.

I knew I had to stand up for my man and see to it that he got the war trophy. I spoke up, and proper protocol was followed.

Lesson learned: A good leader follows orders but must question or stand up to superiors when they act inappropriately—even if it could damage his status. Rank-and-file workers deserve protection from abusive managers who would overstep their authority. Subordinates will return loyalty and support if it is shown for them in prickly circumstances.

Unexploded Bomb or Consider Your Options

As mentioned previously, many days during a patrol were tedious—almost dull and uneventful. Heat, humidity, bugs, difficult terrain, and high stress aside, it could simply be downright tiresome, kind of like work.

However, sometimes, an unusual event occurred where innovation and choices came into the picture. Such was the case when our platoon had orders to reconnoiter an area where a suspected Vietcong base camp had been bombed by the Air Force. We were able to find the area—either through competent map reading and compass work or sheer luck—as normal—likely a bit of both. And sure enough, the enemy had apparently been driven away. There was not any significant bomb damage, and several bunkers were intact. The unique thing was that a five-hundred-pound bomb had failed to explode and was lying almost in the center of the small complex. (At times, US planes flying low-level used a device on bombs that flared out as the ordnance was released, slowing the bomb's descent and allowing the low-flying aircraft to escape the ensuing blast.) Apparently, something must have malfunctioned with this bomb. It was still live.

So the dilemma was what to do with the ordnance that the enemy could potentially use as a booby trap (now known as an IED or improvised explosive device). I radioed battalion tactical operations center (TOC) to advise them and to ask for guidance. After deliberation back at the firebase, our orders came down: use C-4 explosive to detonate the bomb.

My response: "We are not ordnance disposal experts, and we probably don't have enough C-4 (the white "plastic" explosive sometimes used to heat C rations)."

Well, battalion decided to dispatch a Huey with extra C-4 and additional communication wires—as in several hundred feet—for use in connecting blasting caps in the C-4 and one of our PRC 25 radio batteries.

Problem: The helicopter wouldn't arrive until the next day.

So here are the choices: Sleep with the bomb, thus not allowing VC to creep back and booby trap it—but allowing them to know our exact nighttime location and attack on foot or with mortars—or move out and away to a new nighttime position but risk coming back to potential ambush and booby-trapped bomb. (We also discovered a cache of mortar rounds in one of the bunkers and were directed to dispose of them as well, using them to destroy the bunkers.)

Neither option was particularly attractive. After discussion with my platoon sergeant and squad leaders, it was decided we'd stay in the complex. The night passed uneventfully, and we received the additional explosives with instructions to attach the C-4 around the nose of the bomb, insert a blasting cap into the C-4, and back way, way off—as far as our electrical wire allowed. We decided we'd put two blasting caps in the C-4 and splice them to our wire. After moving out and hopefully achieving a suitable cover, it was time to connect or touch the wire to one of our PRC-25 radio batteries. My platoon sergeant had the honors since it was his birthday. He hit the battery terminals with the wire. Nothing. Again. Nothing.

Hmm, had the VC watched us and then gone behind us to disconnect our caps? Was the resistance in the wire due to its length too great? More options to consider. I decided I would take three men and go back to see what could be wrong. Battalion had no answers, and this was truly an OJT (on-the-job training) situation.

When we arrived back at the bomb site, I determined to use only one cap, surmising that possibly the current was too weak to detonate either of the first two we'd inserted.

Back to our cover location and another try. This time, success, and a mighty boom echoed through the jungle. Mission accomplished.

The point of this long war tale is that sometimes new problems pop up, and you have to improvise. No one in our chain of command had performed an act just like this one. And there were elements of risk all around the problem. But patience, innovation, and persistence made it work.

Lesson learned: Prickly problems or unexpected challenges may arise when no team member has had experience. After appropriate consultation, the most sensible decision and an optimal choice must be made. Try to consider potential consequences, but then move forward, adjust as necessary, and achieve your objective.

Attempt to get guidance or answers from good sources first but remember you'll have to decide and ultimately be responsible to execute.

Check Fire! Check Fire! or Stop
Bad Things Immediately

Perhaps one of the most harrowing experiences for me involved friendly fire, which is when your own artillery accidentally hits your position. Mistakes by those of us calling for artillery fire missions and by those executing the artillery fire were certainly possible due to a number of factors. Maps of Vietnam were notoriously inaccurate. Inexperience and poor training were sometimes reasons for botched fire missions.

My incident happened during a mission in War Zone D where A Company was moving as three platoon elements separated by approximately a kilometer each. By this time in my tour, I was confident in my map reading and orienteering skills. I understood topographical features, and our pace counts were reliable.

On the night of the event, my platoon was a flank element with the company commander (CO) in the center platoon. The CO's element suspected enemy movement outside their nighttime position, and the artillery forward observer assigned to them called for a fire mission.

Now one critical issue for artillery fire is whether or not the friendly position lies on the "gun target line" (i.e., between the artillery battery and the target or is on the other side of the target and in the extended trajectory path of the artillery round. Thus, a round fired too short or too long can miss the intended target and impact on the "friendlies").

A 199th SOP (Standard Operating Procedure) was to plot defensive concentrations or defensive targets (Def Cons or Delta Tangos) once nighttime positions were set. These were predetermined potential gun targets that were communicated to the battery and preplotted to be executed more quickly if a platoon was attacked during the night.

In this instance, the forward observer (FO) did not call for a marking round to get a reference point for his position to ensure the platoon was where they thought they were but rather called for a fire mission using one of his DTs. Unfortunately, my platoon was on the gun target line, and the rounds fired hit on top of our position. Chaos and shock followed. My radio telephone operator (RTO), lying right beside me, was hit by 105-mm howitzer shrapnel in the back of his leg. Another soldier caught shrapnel in his M-16 but was unscathed. We, primarily my platoon sergeant, frantically screamed "Check fire! Check fire!" into our PRC-25 radios. This command means to immediately cease firing.

The rounds were stopped, and Specialist Fourth Class Dick Tritt was medevaced out via chopper and sent back to the States to recuperate. We were both lucky and unlucky. No one was killed, and Tritt got home alive and recovered.

I think the FO made a mistake, which could have killed American troops, but I also know the battery could have miscalculated on the fire mission. Or maybe we had misread our position. At any rate, we knew we had to stop any more rounds from being fired, and our yelling was so loud maybe the radio wasn't necessary.

Point is when truly negative or dangerous situations occur, stop them immediately.

Lesson learned: Managers may get a bit slack because an operation seems to just plug along, and he doesn't realize lethargy and inattention to detail are creeping in. But there are times when circumstances are clearly unsafe or illegal and must change immediately. That's when it's okay and imperative for any team member to yell "Check fire!" as soon and as loud as possible.

Unsafe, illegal, or unethical situations must cease as soon as they are identified, even when one is a newly appointed manager. Don't wait until irreparable damage is done in the business unit. Yes, there may be consequences for one's position or career when higher-ups attempt to gloss over or cover up the issue, but never compromise your integrity.

Go Check It Out or Use an Old Pro's Help

Once, after about as pleasant a day as you could spend in Vietnam—we had returned from an in-country R & R visit to the coastal town of Vũng Tàu and were at our large rear brigade main base (BMB)—my good friend Lt. Dave Weimer and I were relaxing, writing letters home. The day had been fun and a welcome respite from missions in the field. We'd showered and looked forward to sleeping on cots in a hootch (slang for small building) before having to return to forward Fire Support Base Libby in the morning.

Our mood was broken by a young trooper banging on the screen door of the company HQ and yelling and babbling about fighting and killing and all sorts of terrible things. He was crying and obviously drunk. The young man was White and was ranting about some sort of Blacks-versus-Whites riot in the barracks nearby. We attempted to calm him down—"They're gonna kill each other!"—and assess the true situation since some racially charged episodes did occur in rear areas.

The company commander just said, "Dick, you and Dave go check it out."

Well, we both knew this was not much different from starting down a trail that you just knew promised an ambush. And damn it, we were in the rear where it was supposed to be safe! And even though all line troopers were required to turn in their weapons when arriving at the brigade main base (BMB) for stand-down, we knew there was a serious threat in those barracks.

I think we both somehow instinctively knew to find our company first sergeant to go with us. Top was big, tough, and experienced. We were average size, not tough, and young. Top piled in a jeep with us—carrying a baseball bat. Oh, my! Why didn't we think of that?

When we arrived at the barracks, things were quiet. We could see damage from a ruckus, and I promise you the tension in the air seemed at least as threatening and scary as anything we'd felt in the deep jungle. We tried to walk in with authority like we knew what we were doing, but it was the presence of the big first sergeant that created a sense of order and discipline. He took charge, and we let him, and we were glad he did. No one was seriously hurt, and people went back to their duties.

Lesson learned: Don't think you can handle all situations alone. You may have the rank and the education but not the experience and respect or savvy. Use associates who know the ropes like the old first sergeant. Get the right kind of help in difficult situations. Use an old pro to help you—don't think that your rank or position will necessarily win the day.

Folks are wise when it comes to smelling a bluff. A young, inexperienced manager is usually seen as just that, but when he/she is supported by a respected vet, then things go smoother. Seasoned supervisors more than likely know the troublemakers and where the risks lie. Listen to them.

Fire Mission, DUSTOFF, Friendships, and Resupply or Rely on the Back Office

We who were in ground units knew we had a tough job—"humping a sack" through thick jungle while trying to stay alert and "close with and destroy the enemy." It was the ultimate challenge. And naturally, we resented the men back in the rear who slept on cots every night, had overhead cover and hot meals, cold beer and showers. We looked down on them, derisively calling them REMFs (rear echelon m— s)—all the while wishing we had similar cushy jobs. And because, in all honesty, since everyone's primary goal was getting home alive, finding a way to get out of the field and into a rear area job was always a top priority.

But, when the stuff hit the fan, the first response after returning fire was to get on "the horn" (radio) to the rear and call for support. Support might mean artillery fire, gunships, or a medevac helicopter (DUSTOFF) if someone was wounded. Quick action on the part of the rear echelon boys was often our salvation. US tactics developed over years of Vietnam battle experience meant after initial engagement, our superior firepower and mobility could almost always win the day. But the guys in the rear had to perform—and they usually did so in great fashion.

There were approximately ten to twelve troopers in the rear supporting each line trooper. Their activities were crucial to the ground units' successful mission completion.

DUSTOFF pilots were especially heroic, often braving enemy ground fire to lift out WIAs. Resupply birds would do all they could to get us our water, food, and extra goodies. We loved those guys.

Lesson learned: Line/field salesmen frequently hold home office staff personnel in low regard, feeling they have no understanding of the challenges in the marketplace. Sometimes, this may be true, but a competent, attentive staff is critical to an organization's success. Leaders must make it clear that staff personnel always put field personnel needs first and that they go the last mile to support frontline efforts.

The perception that those in the home office or "ivory tower" are out of touch or don't care will eventually affect morale, customer service, and satisfaction. Trust between "line troops" and "support troops" is essential to the long-term success of any large organization. And trust comes from reliable, quick response.

Lead Well, Stay Out; Screw Up, Come In or Reward the Right Things

It seems there are many paradoxes in life and even more so in war. One example that was particularly unsettling concerned the effects of leading well versus leading poorly in Vietnam.

The casualty rate for platoon leaders was high in the Vietnam War, not unlike other conflicts. As a leader, the lieutenant was required to be close to the action to best determine appropriate small unit tactics. And the enemy wants to take out leaders.

Training for infantry officers came via West Point, ROTC, or OCS. Some NCOs might be given a battlefield commission, and these individuals had usually gained sufficient experience in the field. Results from training varied, and some individuals were simply natural leaders. Some had better support teams. At any rate, when a lieutenant handled the command of his platoon well, he was given more responsibility. Or, in other words, his unit was asked/ordered to perform more tasks, which usually were more demanding and dangerous since the track record indicated competence and good results. Likewise, the enlisted man/squad member who proved savvy was given more responsibility and authority. No one wanted an incompetent point man or machine gunner, for instance.

So the paradox was that the soldier who did well got to stay out in the bush and lead more dangerous missions because he got desired results. The less capable individual was given "safer" (less responsible) jobs so as not to endanger his mates.

Now this would seem to make some sense, that is, don't allow a goof-up to cause harm. But human nature is such that it soon finds that the knucklehead reduces his risk exposure while the adept person increases his. So the "get him out of there before he gets someone killed" approach, in a way, rewarded ineptitude and kept the good people in harm's way.

Lesson learned: "Screw up and move up" was the old saying. "It's who you know." It can happen in business too. Some managers who seem to just stumble through get the promotion or transfer a much abler person doesn't. Moves like that can really hurt morale and performance. Yes, it may be timing: right place, right time. But a smart leader attempts to control those incidents and reward the person who's really good and has produced over the long haul.

Results matter, yes—but be aware of how they are achieved. For instance, some managers seem successful but simply benefit from a strong market. Make sure you recognize who's really doing a good job and why.

Bad Actors or Put Up with Just So Much

At one point during my tour as a platoon leader, a new troop was assigned to my unit. He had been in a sister company and had had some issues. The story was that during a firefight, he had crawled back from the action and away from his duty as an ammo bearer. It was decided that it was best if he left that platoon and company and got a new start.

The young man was a Black guy, and when I met with him, I found him to be pleasant enough and seemingly willing to be a part of my team. Was the problem racially motivated, perhaps? Was the story of leaving his post in battle true? I simply said we welcomed him to our team and that whatever happened was in the past. He appeared fine with my position/comments.

So, on our first patrol with Smith in the platoon, as we were moving in file (with about our usual number of men, twenty or so), we paused to read the map and get our bearings, and a loud thump occurred behind me and the point element.

What the hell, I thought.

Then, all was quiet, and we moved out trying to maintain good noise discipline. And again as we paused to determine our progress, another loud thump happened. This time, I moved back down the line to find out what was going on. Well, Smith had dropped the ammo can of M-60 machine gun rounds that he was carrying as an ammo bearer—apparently on purpose. I got up in his face and chewed him out for possibly exposing our position. Very odd because the men knew stealth was critical.

That evening, as we were setting up our nighttime position and men were putting out trip flares and claymores, there was some kind of commotion. When I checked it out, one troop was kind of snickering and told me to ask his squad leader about it. Well, as it turned out, Smith would not go out far enough from his position to properly place the flare and claymore, and the sergeant took exception to the point of getting physical with Smith.

Now the benefit of the doubt was gone. Smith had issues.

The final straw came after we returned to Firebase Gladys and had a couple of days to prepare for our next patrol. As I was getting the platoon set to move out, the medic said Smith was refusing to go because of a foot problem. Was it real?

The medic said not, and I confronted Smith about his alleged ailment. He just said he couldn't/ wouldn't go out with us.

Enough was enough. I went to our CO and said Smith was not going to be my problem anymore. My platoon was not going to be endangered by his actions or outright cowardice. So since he was refusing to go into the field, it meant a trip to LBJ (Long Binh Jail) and a court-martial. It was his decision: jail versus going in harm's way.

Lesson learned: Everyone deserves the benefit of the doubt—at least once. They deserve a chance to fit in and work with the team. But after having legitimate opportunities, their failings cannot be allowed to endanger the team's mission. Smith made his choice, just as work world Smiths will make theirs in selfish ways that can damage your business goals. Know when it's time to cut someone loose who is detrimental to achieving your mission.

River Mission to Place Sensors or What?

As I hope some of my reflections have shown, there were some odd and quirky episodes during my tour. Another such incident happened while our company was operating out of Firebase Gladys on the banks of the Song Dong Nai River in War Zone D.

During the Vietnam War, new surveillance technology came into use. One such type of equipment involved sensors, which, after being buried near known enemy trails, could pick up vibrations caused by movement of troops (or wildlife). The sensors were not large and would be placed just off a trail unnoticeably to transmit detected activity back to a receiving station. And in free-fire zones such as War Zone D, artillery fire could then be called in on the area under surveillance. Free-fire zones meant there were no villages or no known activity from civilians in the area, so it was assumed anyone there was enemy.

Our intel types decided that we should deploy sensors on a trail upriver from Gladys. There were various trail networks in the area—hard-packed from use by VC and NVA in moving through the area of operations (AO) and almost undetectable from the air due to thick jungle canopy.

The issue was how to get to the trail to be observed. It was probably at least two klicks (kilometers) away through dense jungle, and we would have a couple of intel types with us.

At the firebase, we had a sixteen-foot johnboat with an outboard motor. We used it to ferry men across the river periodically since it was about fifty meters wide during the rainy season at the Gladys location. So it was decided that I would take along two men and the "spooks" on a boat trip to where the trail crossed the river upstream.

It is still hard to fathom that we would load up a small aluminum boat and travel totally exposed up a river and then just land it with no cover on the stream bank. It was also hard to believe we could pinpoint where the trail met the river, for that matter, but we did.

I had an M-60 machine gunner with me, and as we traveled along, I wondered if we should just rake the riverside with fire before we beached or simply hit the shore. Automatic weapon fire would surely announce our arrival, but we could be seen or heard all along our route anyway! I decided against firing.

We scrambled ashore and moved down the trail a distance from the river. The intel techie planted several devices near the well-traveled trail, and we moved back to our boat and back down the river. Mission accomplished.

This tactic allowed for a type of remote, unmanned kind of ambush. However, it could be indiscriminate in that a wayward pig or water buffalo could set off sensors and bring quite a shell shower on wildlife.

Sometimes, an idea seems pretty good, but if not for sheer luck, bad things may happen.

Lesson learned: Companies may get seemingly bright ideas for a new product or customer program. But implementation could be problematic, and what seemed to offer promising results might turn ugly. Make sure potential pitfalls are considered and do not take unnecessary risks versus expected rewards. Collateral damage can be difficult to overcome when customers or employees perceive recklessness. And sufficient test marketing can reduce chances for failure.

No Air Mattress or Same Rules Apply

"Rank has its privileges" is an old saying, and I suppose many folks believe it's a military thing. But it can be said that rank has its responsibilities too. Rank or grade is something that is achieved in the military through effort, training, and perseverance. It must be handled judiciously if proper trust and respect are to be realized, leading to positive responses from troops.

On one mission, Second Platoon was operating with our company commander and his four-man team (RTO, forward artillery observer and his RTO). This captain was on his second tour in Vietnam and was pretty gung ho, tough and confident. My platoon had a standard operating procedure (SOP) that stated no air mattress use for sleeping unless it was really raining hard. This policy was in effect because air mattresses made noise whenever you rolled over on them, potentially divulging a nighttime position. And they caused a trooper to be higher off the ground and thus more vulnerable to small arms fire or shrapnel. Neither did I allow hammocks for sleeping except in extremely rainy conditions.

On a particular night with the captain, he admonished me to keep better noise discipline with the platoon. I passed this on to my squad leaders for dissemination to the troops. One outspoken sergeant took issue with the captain's observation—he'd be glad to comply if the captain would quit making so much damn noise with his inflated air mattress!

Another old saying is "What's good for the goose is good for the gander." People know these things. You want me to do something that you don't or won't do? Uh-uh. If there are reasonable rules, then they apply to all, and the leader has the most responsibility to follow them first, especially if serious consequences may occur.

Lesson learned: Don't expect your people to follow rules ostensibly meant for everyone if you're not going to. Hypocrisy or abuse of perceived privilege irritates people about as much as anything. It creates a "them and us" gap that leads to dysfunction and contention.

When a business leader is seen coming in late or believed to get more perks than are reasonable, employees take note, and resentment may build. Lead by example.

Walk Point or Lead by Example

The point man performed arguably the most important—and dangerous—function for a platoon on patrol. This function involved being the first man to walk in the file, leading the rest of the group through the jungle. He would be first to see the enemy—and likely to be seen by him. It took individuals with skill and courage to "agree" to become point men. We needed men who were able to maintain a reasonable pace in different, difficult types of terrain, stay on the compass heading, and, most of all, act as the first eyes, ears, and—yes—nose of the platoon. The job had to be done with as much stealth as possible in the thick jungle while staying ready to "outdraw" a surprised VC or NVA adversary.

Imagine attempting to break through thick vegetation quietly while avoiding snakes and fire ants and knowing that your next step could bring the explosion of a booby trap or small arms fire and, with it, death or serious injury. Most of the men in my platoon who walked point held rank below a sergeant's. Yet they were leaders in the truest sense.

Sometimes, the platoon sergeant or platoon leader might walk point. It may have been because he was trying to set an example or the other designated point man simply wouldn't go in harm's way at that particular time. It might have been to show the men that movement had to be faster or just to have a new point man. Most of the training was OJT (on-the-job training), and there were never enough good point men. One of ours—who we nicknamed Hillbilly—could seemingly smell the bad guys. He was a Georgia country boy who wasn't scared, was a little wild, and had the confidence of the platoon—good ol' boy who was a leader.

My significant point story occurred during the incursion into Cambodia in 1970. The enemy had indeed used that place as a sanctuary and for reserves of supplies. It seemed that every patrol turned up more arms and matériel. My platoon was ordered to follow up on an aerial reconnaissance, which had indicated a sighting of containers, crates, and other items. I was reluctant to follow the order because our numbers were down to thirteen men, and I did not want to encounter a larger, well-armed force. But we moved out after losing the "discussion" with our CO.

From fortuitous map reading and compass work, we came to the area where the helicopter scouts had made the sighting. The problem: a stream between us and the location. Now stream crossings were dangerous because of the exposure and length of time to cross the open area. This particular one also required navigating fairly steep banks. I took the point—after deploying appropriate security upstream and downstream to protect our flanks. So I was the lead man into the waist-deep water and first to come up the bank on the other side because I felt I had to lead by example. Thank goodness no bad guys were around at the time. We checked out the site and found only old, empty crates—another example of "worker bees" performing a task thought necessary by managers who were a bit removed from the situation. Fortunately, my team suffered no harm, and perhaps they realized I too would be willing to go in harm's way even when I disagreed with the order.

Lesson learned: Be prepared and willing to set an example by doing a dirty job at times so your team understands you would not ask them to do something that you wouldn't be ready to perform yourself. If associates know the boss will step into a difficult situation or regularly visit the work area, they will have a much more positive and productive attitude.

A fine example in my business unit was when a plant manager would spell line workers on one of the most demanding jobs to give the associate a break and to show the manager was willing to get his hands dirty.

This will build trust and respect, and it will allow you as a leader to better appreciate what your associates face every day.

General on the Scene—Let Me Know if I Can Help

In the segment on "Only Because We Like You," I reference the extended firefight Second Platoon experienced and the fire support activities ranging from Huey gunships, Air Force jets, ammunition resupply, and the brigade commander's presence.

This anecdote concerns how General William Bond handled the situation where one of his subordinates was locked in a prolonged firefight. General Bond was a "soldier's soldier" and exhibited the traits I discuss in the book. He was the only US general to die in the Vietnam War on the ground as a result of hostile fire.

As previously discussed, Second Platoon had run into an enemy element, which was dug in, and was willing to fight more tenaciously than what normally occurred in our AO. Usually, after initial contact and sporadic firing, the enemy attempted to slip away, knowing that we would call in artillery or gunships and possibly airlift in more troops as well.

On this day, since the firing continued, there was more radio communication between myself and support elements. General Bond could hear this communication aboard his command and control (C and C) helicopter. He arrived overhead in our vicinity to observe the action. During a lull in radio traffic, he contacted me using his call sign—which gave me an aha moment even under the circumstances. This was the big kahuna on the net!

Second lieutenants are used to having pretty much everyone from specialist fours to colonels telling them what they should do. But this day, the 199th Brigade commander simply told me he was present, what armament he had available to me on his chopper, and to advise if I wanted his help.

He let me know—in the right manner—that I was in charge on the ground and that I could call for whatever support was available, including him. It was a real confidence builder, and it truly made me respect General Bond's approach to leading his men.

Lesson learned: Field managers don't want to be micromanaged. They want leeway to conduct business the way their local market demands. Now that doesn't mean they shouldn't follow corporate policy or do things unethically or think they outright own their operation. It means that a good leader will trust the "guy on the ground" to best understand what's really happening and what kind of support will help the most in delivering goals in a certain market and then ensure that help is forthcoming within reasonable limits.

Stand Down or Give It a Rest

I t's certainly an understatement to say that combat patrols in Vietnam were stressful. Our missions to "seek out and destroy" the enemy could last anywhere from three or four days to over two weeks. And believe me, moving through thick jungle in a tropical climate, not knowing if an ambush lay ahead, can be very stressful.

Combine that kind of life-and-death uncertainty with what seemed to be ever-changing timelines (i.e., the mission is extended for three more days in the boonies), and you've got troops who really begin to need a break.

Typical missions might average six or so days; that is, a platoon spent six days patrolling, setting ambushes, etc. before returning to base camp. The unit would remain in a fire support base (FSB) for maybe two days and nights before returning to areas of operation (AOs) where enemy activity was suspected. The time in a firebase, while better than being in the jungle, didn't provide a lot of creature comforts.

So the Army devised "stand-downs" to be held approximately every forty-five to fifty days. A stand-down meant the company would return to a larger and more secure rear area—a main base— for four to five days of rest. It meant good showers, sleeping on a cot, electricity, maybe a trip to the PX, a steak fry, calls home via MARS2 radio hookups, a Filipino band, and a whole bunch of cold beer. Practical issues such as small arms maintenance/repairs and administrative record updating also occurred.

By the end of three days, some troops were so hung over they almost welcomed a return to the forward firebases and the business of war.

Lesson learned: Business can be stressful too. We may forget that we consistently ask our people to do more with less—to "stay out in the field" a little longer. Over time, this creates friction, weariness, and maybe attitude and performance problems.

So think about the "stand-down." How can you periodically allow employees to relax, celebrate, and recharge their batteries? It may be something as simple as a company picnic. It may be offering tickets to a concert or ball game. But all the folks need a break every few months. Make sure they know that you know that and then show them with an event or gesture that conveys your concern and appreciation for their efforts.

Your team can get tired—both mentally and physically. Let them know you care and understand. Allow them to rest and recharge periodically. Celebrations/stand-downs don't have to be expensive affairs. Chili cook-offs, barbecues, and a local band after work can relieve the stress.

Swamp Surprise or Sometimes No Place to Hide

Each mission our platoon worked presented some unique experience for us young men. Soon after A Company was assigned a new CO, we were designated for a deeper insertion into a jungle area bordering AO Wichita. The plan was to have the entire company move from a remote LZ toward the open, cultivated areas where I had first been introduced to enemy contact. Our old CO seemed to have a knack for keeping us in the more open fields than patrolling in the "J" for "Juliet" or "jungle" where we didn't feel we had an advantage with our firepower and air cover. This time, we were going in from the backside, if you will, instead of probing into the jungle from the open area or simply waiting in fields for bad guys to come out of the "J."

Our LZ (landing zone) was small but adequate to get A Company inserted and onto our patrol. We immediately found that our route of travel took us into a low-lying area that wasn't evident from maps or air recon, and thus, we were moving in water sometimes ankle- to waist-deep. Our maps were not very reliable. It made for tough, slow movement because of the vegetation and roots below the surface, not to mention the usual vines and growth you could see.

The main goal of our first day was to find enough dry ground to set a nighttime position. We finally found an area that sufficed and spent a relatively quiet night. The next day, Second Platoon was due to be on point. We moved out, and it wasn't long before the CO prodded us via radio to pick up the pace. As mentioned, the going was tough in the swampy conditions. Our captain decided Third

Platoon could make better progress and had them slog past Second to take the lead. We took some razzing as they edged past us. Third Platoon did move a bit quicker, and it wasn't long before their point man spotted some higher ground and began to make his way out of our watery trail. Probably three men from the Third were onto dry ground when all hell broke loose. We had stumbled directly on a small VC base camp almost like we had zeroed in on it.

Well, there was nowhere to take cover except underwater for the lead element. The rest of us tried to turn and backtrack. Rounds were flying from the VC camp and clipping leaves and limbs. It was a mad scramble, and I don't know if any US troop fired a shot unless it was our point man. It was possible that since we were lower in the swampy area, that enemy small arms fire flew high. One Third Platoon member had a round go right through his helmet, literally almost giving him a new part down the middle of his scalp. Other men twisted ankles and got scratched up, but no one was wounded by weapons fire.

The FO (forward observer) immediately called for a fire mission, and we waited as the big guns did their thing. We tried to put ordnance down in a manner that would create casualties for the fleeing enemy. After sufficient shelling, we cautiously moved back up into the base camp. No body count but we had disrupted their little "home." It would take time for Charlie to regroup and restock anywhere near.

Our plan was basically sound: get behind the competition and surprise him. We met some unexpected difficulties. We made a change to see if we could progress faster. We were fortunate with our discovery/success but again met difficulty. In the end, the mission succeeded but partly due to some dumb luck.

Once again, fate had been kind. Did my slowness due to inexperience save the Second from injury or death? Were the men of the Second just lucky? Why did we find the needle in a swampy haystack, anyway?

Lesson learned: Businesses can have similar situations. Have a good plan, persist, adjust, and maybe you'll get lucky. Unforeseen circumstances will occur, so be as ready as you can.

Sometimes, you do the best you can, yet circumstances allow you nowhere to go. All you can do is hunker down. It doesn't mean you stay hunkered down—you take steps that are available (e.g., call for appropriate support). And you give thanks that things went okay.

Only Because We Like You or Respect and Affection versus Fear and Intimidation

t bothers and frustrates me to watch movies and TV programs that generally portray military officers or CEOs as tough, gruff screamers. They seem to almost always be portrayed as abusive, bossy, and unsympathetic or total tyrants with no clue or empathy. Good leaders are not like that at all. Sure, there are times for tough, direct comments, and zero tolerance for truly bad behavior is a good characteristic. But management by fear and intimidation just won't get it done in the long run.

This belief can be exhibited via one of my platoon's most significant actions during my tour. I had been sent from a patrol to the battalion aid station to have an abscess on my jaw lanced and cleaned. I had left just a day before our platoon was to be airlifted to a small mountain for a recon mission. The area had not been actively patrolled, and recent intelligence reports indicated a potentially dangerous situation. I had mixed feelings about not being on the initial insertion with the platoon but knew that, left to fester, the abscess could become a pretty significant health issue. So our battalion doc lanced the infected area on my jaw and, instead of suturing the incision, packed it with string gauze so it could heal from the inside out. (Clogged pores and resultant infections were frequent concerns due to lengthy jungle patrols and consequent hygiene conditions.) While an unpleasant procedure, I figured to have a couple of days in Firebase Libby to allow the doc to monitor my healing before I had to return to the platoon.

Well, of course, the guys made contact on the mountain right away, discovering a VC base camp and killing one of the enemy. The tactical operations center officer (TOC) notified me the battalion wanted me to rejoin my team ASAP since they had no officer with them. I, with a large white bandage covering the side of my face, demurred, fearing infection and selfishly thinking, *Geez, what about my slack time!* (Fine leadership thoughts.) A quick call by the TOC to the medical officer and his okay for me to hop on a chopper followed.

Back with my platoon, I assessed the situation and found a dead VC and a scattered bunker complex that indicated, as suspected, the enemy was using the area to stage incursions into nearby villages and to set ambushes. Since the men had dropped their rucksacks for easier movement upon finding the camp and engaging the enemy, I sent one squad back to recover the gear and return it so we could secure the base camp area and continue to check out the surroundings and prepare for nighttime laager.

The path to the gear led them into more bunkers and an ambush. Five men were wounded although none seriously. We returned fire and called for a medevac for the wounded. The firefight was more long lived and intense than usual. We had to call for ammunition resupply. Eventually, I directed Huey gunships and worked with an Air Force Forward Air Controller (FAC) to direct an F-100 bomb drop on the enemy position. Our brigade commander, General Bond, arrived on the scene in his command chopper and offered assistance.

Long story shortened, we spent the night halfway down the mountain after evacuating four men. One WIA stayed the night with an AK-47 round in his leg. The next day, after moving off the mountain, we received some replacement troops, and I proceeded to direct extensive artillery fire onto the enemy position. And as expected, battalion ordered us back up the mountain to assess damage and determine if the enemy was gone. Upon hearing the order, the men very nicely said, "We ain't goin' back up there!" They had seen five buddies wounded and didn't relish going again against a dug-in adversary.

Now this is where the yelling and threatening "get your ass in gear" stuff doesn't work well, in my opinion. Their feelings were understandable. Hell, I felt the same way—and I told them so. I believe they appreciated my candor and realized that we had an obligation to follow orders. But I asked rather than ordered. After getting agreement, one of the machine gunners said, "You know, sir, we wouldn't do this if we didn't like you."

The results of our return are another story.

Lesson learned: Most really good leaders are not the wild, profane bullies we've been shown in movies. They are competent and strong but generally empathetic. They gain respect and trust through the integrity of their behavior and perform as necessary under duress. They can get their team to respond when times are difficult, and the mission is distasteful.

When a business faces tough times, threats of layoffs, closures, and salary cuts will not necessarily drive positive behavior. Difficult situations require a team approach. "We're in this mess together— let's get on with the hard work. Here's our plan."

Jeep Wreck or Control Your Focus

After a trip from Fire Support Base Libby back to the brigade main base at Long Binh for some duty—possibly acting as paymaster, I cannot remember exactly—I had to return to Libby. Transportation was by jeep including a driver, another enlisted man, and myself riding shotgun.

The route to Libby included some miles on Highway 1, arguably the main road in South Vietnam. It wove through villages and uninhabited countryside and was generally fairly safe in our area of operations.

On this particular trip, the three of us were traveling along with no issues. But in one of the towns, an old black French Citroën with some ARVN (Army of the Republic of Vietnam) soldiers roared past us and stopped a ways ahead. We drove past it. Later, they passed us again, and we determined they were screwing with the Americans. So we began to pay more attention.

In fact, my driver became overly focused on them as they were parked on the left side of the road up ahead. He apparently was worried they might pull out right in front of us. He developed a "target fixation."

I realized this and also noticed a flatbed truck stopped in front of us about a hundred yards on the edge of our side of the road. *Surely, he sees it*, I thought. By the time I realized he did not notice it was stopped, we were right up on it, going too fast. I yelled "Watch out!" and grabbed the steering wheel to turn us left. He jammed on the brakes, and we rammed up under the truck bed, knocking the jeep's windshield down on us in the front seat. We were lucky not to have been beheaded.

Thankfully, we only had minor scratches and high heart rates. The Vietnamese truck driver jabbered away, and the ARVNs were gone.

Close call for sure.

Lesson learned: Pay attention to what's going on in your work area. Be aware of potential problems and prepare for necessary action. Do not become so focused on the potential problem that you miss another, which could be even worse. And it's wise to have colleagues assisting you in your duties—copilots, so to speak, who can "grab the wheel" if needed. Remember, there may be a chance someone's screwing with you and distracting from your primary goal: reaching your destination safely.

Sad Duty or Show Empathy

Units of our sister battalion, the Fourth of the Twelfth, were engaged in a large firefight with NVA forces and took more than normal casualties. Multiple medevacs were needed. During the operations, some standard operating procedures (SOPs) were skirted, such as allowing killed-in-action casualties (KIAs) to be lifted out on the same helicopter as wounded-in-action troops (WIAs). This was not normal procedure as it was believed wounded troops were adversely affected by having dead comrades next to them on the flight to hospitals.

In this incident, the medevac bird had lifted off with the crew and the wounded and a KIA when it was hit by rocket-propelled grenade (RPG) fire and, either in attempting to maneuver or losing control, the body of the KIA fell from the chopper as it was going down.

Afterward, in searching for the wreckage and remains, the body couldn't be found. Technically, this meant it was missing-in-action (MIA) since it had not been recovered. It was SOP never to leave any remains behind. Our enemy knew this and, at times, would wait to ambush us as we returned to search.

Some weeks or more later, the body was found by a 5/12 unit— or at least what remains were left. There were just some bones, dog tags, and, oddly, the trooper's plastic 199th LIB wallet. These wallets had our unit patch on the front and had sealable "pages" inside for pictures.

Somehow, I was tasked with getting the remains back to our Long Binh BMB. They were bundled up in a poncho and felt like they (the bones) weighed about five pounds. I carried the "package" to BMB and turned it in to the proper people for further disposition.

It was an odd feeling to carry what had once been a young American soldier who had served his country and then to just be unceremoniously dropped off.

Lessons learned: Strange things are going to occur at some point. You may be required to be involved in some way. And while in your secret heart, you are glad it wasn't your time, you must have empathy and respect for the victim.

It may entail visiting a colleague in the hospital after a diagnosis of terminal cancer or going to see the spouse of a coworker who committed suicide as I once had to do. But it means having empathy and compassion. While doing what may seem uncomfortable, good leaders step up and treat others in difficult times as they would like to be treated.

Welcome Back, Lieutenant Rose, or They're Nice When They Need You

I n Vietnam, second lieutenants who led platoons were looked upon with, I feel, a combination of doubt and respect. Newcomers were untested and represented a risk to men and mission until they had a baptism by fire. It seemed that some colonels and captains sort of treated "butter bars" (second lieutenants) with disdain or like the junior-most officers that they were. But after time in the field and promotion to first lieutenant, more courtesy and trust began to emerge.

After spending six months as platoon leader of the Second Platoon, A Company, Fifth Battalion, Twelfth Infantry of the 199th Light Infantry Brigade (Separate), I received my promotion to first lieutenant. I had been in the Army for almost two years. And better yet, I was getting a position in the TOC (tactical operations center) at a forward fire support base and going on R & R to Australia! Things were working out pretty well, it seemed.

Of course, there's always a twist. While in Australia on R & R, the big news came that President Nixon was sending US troops into Cambodia. While this incursion created an uproar, it was entirely correct and logical. The enemy had been using Cambodia as a sanctuary and supply depot and thumbed their noses at our forces when we stopped short of the border. *Whew*, I thought, *the battalion's going in under the operational control of the First Cavalry Division (Air Mobile), and it ain't going to be pretty, and I'm out of the field!* While there is always some compassion for those who are still in the field, it's human nature to relish one's own seeming good fortune.

Upon returning from R & R to Firebase Libby and a skeleton crew at that base, I felt the good Lord was looking after me. Only a few captains and lieutenants in the firebase, overhead cover, hot meals, etc., and no hairy patrols in the Cambodian jungle.

It lasted about three days. Then the word came in from Cambodia that the First Platoon leader had been injured, and I was to report there immediately to take over while he recuperated. I was convinced that my luck had run out. Our battalion had been involved in one of the bloodiest fights in the early action in Cambodia, and things were a lot more dangerous than what our unit had experienced in Vietnam. Plus I didn't know the platoon, and they didn't really know me.

After a circuitous journey from FSB Libby via BMB Long Binh up to the jump-off spot in Sông Bé and a chopper ride over to Cambodia, I was back in it big time. The firebase in Cambodia was not much—low berm and muddy—and the tactical operations center (TOC) was a hole in the ground with PSP (perforated steel planking) covered in sandbags overhead. I remember it was dusk when I stumbled in and reported. The battalion CO greeted me in a more friendly and nervous manner than usual.

"Glad to see you, Lieutenant Rose."

Well, I thought, *he's never been so courteous but now he needed me.*

B Company was down to about a third of its normal strength, and my company, A, was weak too.

After the pleasantries, I searched out my new platoon and tried to cobble together some gear so I could go on patrols.

My point is that now things were really dicey—only days before the little firebase had been the scene of a horrific battle resulting in over a hundred NVA KIA and the bodies buried in a mass grave. Things had been close for the 5/12 Battalion of the 199th LIB, and every able-bodied troop was critical to complete the mission. But you have to always act like your people are needed and important—not just when the going is tough.

Lesson learned: Make sure all your team feels wanted and welcome—in good times and bad. Sincerity and appreciation for performance are always in vogue. Good leaders make workers feel needed all the time. When associates don't see appreciation, it eventually shows in attitude and work results.

"That's My Best Friend" or Really Serious Things

As mentioned earlier, Cambodia was a difficult place. But that didn't mean GIs didn't want some beer. In fact, since we rarely got beer, we wanted it even more. After I'd turned command of First Platoon back over to the regular platoon leader and was pulling duty in the tactical operations center (TOC), in FSB Myron, things became more tedious versus stressful.

We settled into somewhat of a routine, albeit active with enemy contacts, and knew better what to expect. So where's the beer? We just weren't getting the attention or support from the First Cavalry in terms of amenities like beer since we were "op conned" under operational control to that larger division.

As the discussion about how good a beer would taste went on, I volunteered to ride a supply chopper back into Vietnam and bring back a few cases of suds. While I knew it was somewhat hazardous, it seemed like a good idea at the time.

When I hopped onto a Huey bound for Sông Bé, there were a couple of enlisted men on also—and a body bag holding a young KIA American. One of the grunts was accompanying the body. It was wedged against the seat bracket behind our feet, and after we took off—flying at treetop level to thwart ground fire—the young man next to me said, with tears in his eyes, "That's my best friend." He had been allowed to accompany the body back and see that his buddy was accorded proper treatment. And I was on a beer run. I felt like crap. This young man truly felt devotion to a fallen comrade in arms—something that doesn't get the spin it should regarding Vietnam vets. And I was on a beer run. I felt guilty and petty.

I tried to console the trooper but knew it was futile. He was just heartbroken. Oftentimes, in Vietnam, when someone else was hurt or killed, you felt guilt but also relief that it just wasn't your time. But this fine young man felt a huge sense of loss for an obviously close and dear friend.

Lesson learned: We have serious events in business too along with frivolous occurrences. We must know the difference. A money-losing month is bad—but it's not death. An industrial accident is truly serious—especially if an employee is badly injured or killed. We can always make up for a bad profit month—we can't bring a dead associate back to life.

Understand the difference between really serious events and things that can be rectified. Learn how to prioritize and how to deal with true catastrophes.

When you put the two into proper perspective, you will make better decisions for the long run, and associates will appreciate your actions.

Lead from the Rear or Last Jeep to Hàm Tân

After the battalion completed its mission in Cambodia and some much-deserved stand-down time at the 199th Long Binh BMB, we were ordered to set up a new forward firebase. It meant leaving the familiar surroundings of FSB Libby and going closer to the coast into Bình Tuy Province. A village named Hàm Tân was across a shallow valley from the high ground where we were to construct a base dubbed Deeble—named after one of the lieutenants in our unit who had been killed in action.

Libby would not be dismantled but turned over to the ARVN (Army of the Republic of Vietnam). We would leave the bunkers and facilities for them and move our equipment to the new location. This meant we'd run a convoy from Long Binh to Hàm Tân, and it would take a full day over generally decent roadways (for Vietnam).

We traveled in jeeps and deuce-and-a-halves, and other wheeled vehicles. And as it turned out, I was in the very last jeep in the long procession.

One strange coincidence along our route was when we had to stop, for some reason, and other US vehicles came past—including a jeep carrying my old buddy, Artillery Officer Richard Watson. We had met our first week in-country and hadn't seen each other for about nine or ten months. We just stopped our jeeps and caught up on things.

But there was a schedule to keep, and we were on our radio frequently to prod everyone to keep up and use proper spacing to reduce potential ambush threats. Of course, it was not surprising that we got strung out—several bridges were out, and it took a while to cross streams. So the day dragged on, and it began to get dark.

Nighttime travel on roads where we were headed was not advisable. And we—my jeep with three aboard—were the cow's tail. The first elements reached Hàm Tân, and we were still miles (klicks/kilometers, as we measured distances) away. We had to use our headlights to see the road, and that meant exposing ourselves to potential VC or NVA roadside ambushes. Finally, a helicopter was sent up to fly over for us, in effect showing the enemy a gunship was airborne and could respond to any funny stuff.

We finally rolled into Hàm Tân with no kind of shelter—guys were sleeping in the deuce-and-a-halves and under them. And of course, it began to rain. While we felt relatively confident that there would be no attack, we still didn't have good security. And we were exhausted. I ended up finding a table in the marketplace that was under a canopy and just crawled on top of it with my web gear, helmet, and M-16 and slept. I was awakened in the morning by Vietnamese villagers coming into the marketplace. Talk about exposure and slack security—we sure had it that night. Luckily, it was a friendly village.

Lesson Learned: I'm not sure if describing this episode as leading is accurate, but by bringing up the rear, we exhibited chutzpah if nothing else. Somebody had to be exposed in the tail end Charlie position, and it was us. There can be "back markers" in business too, and they can be important in ensuring things finish well. Don't forget the associates who do cleanup jobs.

At times, we can find ourselves in a role, which, while part of a plan, is sort of shaky. All you can do is make the best of it and try to "keep up" at some point. And management needs to provide cover/support as best it can. Obviously, it is desirable to cover as many bases as possible so team members don't have to crawl onto a table for rest, but at least, recognize associates' sacrifices and make up for shortcomings where possible.

Twenty-Five Thousand Dollars US Cash or Truth in Reporting

s the duty officer in the tactical operations center (TOC) in our battalion forward fire support base, I received pretty much all the reports from units patrolling in the field. Most were routine check-ins or requests for supplies and the like. Of course, when enemy contact was made, things really popped because we channeled artillery and gunship and medical evacuation requests to the proper responders.

One unusual event during my time as TOC officer concerned a platoon's contact with VC and discovery of documents and cold, hard cash in the enemy base camp.

It was a lot of cash: twenty-five thousand dollars in large US bills, up to five hundred dollars denominations. Funds which the enemy (VC) could use on the black market for supplies and to bribe village officials. The platoon leader reported the findings, and we were amazed—wondering how US currency came to be out in the Vietnam jungle and, even more shocking, that the guys turned it over. Well, a few days or a week later, a VC courier was killed by another platoon. He was carrying information about our earlier attack and the loss of money and documents. Our intel report, however, noted the VC claimed more than twenty-five thousand dollars had been lost in the raid. So I was tasked with questioning the lieutenant about the discrepancy. I asked; he replied, "I turned it all in." End of story to my way of thinking, and I so reported.

I didn't hear more until a month or two later when word came out the lieutenant had flashed a five-hundred-dollar bill around.

Nothing more came of the incident, and who knows what the actual outcome was for the money, which was turned in? But I believe that US currency of very high denominations had the serial numbers recorded. If so, when the five-hundred-dollar note was passed/cashed, then the feds would know about it. Thus, the lieutenant could've been questioned and maybe have faced problems.

Lesson learned: The point is that it's best to be honest and factual in your business reporting. There is no telling if or when some odd, unexpected information could surface and do harm (or set the story straight). And don't get cute or braggadocios about something you think you've achieved.

Be forthcoming, not cute or disingenuous. Things have a way of surfacing in the long run, which could prove detrimental to you.

Three-Week Drop or Have Faith in the System

s I've recounted, most of my tour in Vietnam was spent in the field—seven months total as a platoon leader and approximately three and a half months in forward firebases as a tactical operations officer. My last month or so was in the "rear" adjacent to one of the largest US installations in Vietnam. The 199th's brigade main base (BMB) in Long Binh was pretty nice by Vietnam standards. Some facilities were even air-conditioned. And there was an officer's club that provided real cheap drinks, steaks, movies, and occasional live entertainment.

When orders came down that the 199th would be returning to the States, we were ecstatic. Part of President Nixon's Vietnamization Program meant our little unit's mission was almost complete. It also meant that some "drops" or early rotations to the US for some men could occur. (Anyone with six months or more to serve on the 365-day tour would be reassigned to remaining units.) Since, upon our return, the 199th would be deactivated at Fort Benning, Georgia, we would need an advance team to make arrangements for the ceremony.

I heard that a lieutenant who had been with our headquarters company—rear area staff position—was being tabbed to go with the advance group, getting over a week or two lead on the rest of the brigade members. Needless to say, this news was irritating. REMFs (not a nice term) should not get precedence over field troops. I voiced my displeasure to no one in particular, but our battalion commander either heard about it or realized the oversight, he called me into his command bunker and informed me, "Lieutenant Rose, we had planned to send Lieutenant X back with the advance party. But you've been in the field. He hasn't. So I'm changing orders and sending you." Boom. Done. A leader had understood the right thing to do. The system worked.

I had not had faith because, so many times, it seemed the guys in the rear got all the breaks, and field troops got the raw deals. But this proved that when you did the tough jobs as required, it could pay off—as long as your leader was a good one. (And there may need to be a little bit of appropriate complaining.)

Lesson learned: Do your job well and consistently, and over time, your efforts will be recognized. Good leaders must make sure they support the workers who are removed from the home office limelight. A cushy job can be a sort of reward in itself. The dirty jobs must be rewarded specifically or no one will sign up for them. And sometimes, it can help to bring the situation to the right person's attention.

Overbearing Officer or Gimme a Break

This episode occurred after my return from Vietnam to Fort Benning for the retirement ceremony for our unit's colors. The 199th LIB (Sep) was pulled out of Vietnam in the fall of 1970 as part of President Nixon's Vietnamization Program. The brigade had served in country since 1966 with distinction, being awarded both Presidential and Valorous Unit citations.

As I wrote in a previous chapter, I was part of the advance party sent to Fort Benning to ensure things were right for our ceremony at the base. The main body of returning 199th Redcatchers arrived about a week or so after I got to the base. We practiced and drilled for the ceremony, which gave us at least some sense of positive recognition for our service.

The paradox was that while we were back in "the world," we had had to spend time at Benning while very anxious to get back to homes and family. And it meant adherence to more strict stateside US Army routines. Certainly, there were rules in the unit in-country (Vietnam) but not so much when in the field. Rear areas like Long Binh meant wearing the uniform "by the book," saluting, and so on. At Benning, it was back to the old strict Army discipline.

We were treated pretty well at Benning—befitting returning veterans of the war. Officers housed in a BOQ (bachelors officers' quarters) and the enlisted men and NCOs in former OCS barracks. In fact, they were put in the same building, which had been my OCS quarters in '68 to '69. What a coincidence.

It was a good homecoming for me since I got to reunite with some of the officers I'd worked with as an instructor on the tactics committee at the Infantry School after I was commissioned. Back then, I was a new second lieutenant—"butter bar"—who caught grief from all the guys who'd been to Nam and really knew their stuff. It was a good postgrad experience for me, provided by men who had served in almost all our Vietnam combat units.

Our retirement ceremony came off well, I think. I acted as adjutant and had to give various commands for the actual ceremony, such as "Pass in review!" and "Eyes right!"

Best of all, soon after all was completed, we were free to go home on leave or, in some cases, be discharged. There were buses to take guys to the airport for flights out of Columbus to various points, mostly Atlanta. So as men were getting lined up and ready to board buses, you can imagine the excitement. And back then, troops had to travel commercially wearing class A uniforms—no fatigues. We were wearing our dress greens, able to display our ribbons and awards.

Well, it was helter-skelter as jubilant men rushed to get to buses. One Redcatcher was running along without his uniform jacket buttoned all the way—just excited to be going home. As he ran, a major drove up to him and yelled out the car window, berating him for being "out of uniform." The trooper was bewildered and shocked at being chewed out by the senior officer. I came up to try to calm the major, explaining our situation. In my mind, it was clearly an overreaction on his part, and while technically correct, there was an extenuating circumstance in that the young man had just returned from Vietnam and was eager to get home. Got the point made, but the major was still a jerk. Not a great way to treat a young Vietnam combat vet.

Lesson learned: There are times to strongly enforce rules, and there are times to give folks a break. The major was a staff guy—the trooper was a field guy who was lucky to be back alive. His "indiscretion" was minor, and the major should have gently reprimanded him, at worst. The same goes for associates dealing with any myriad of issues. Everyone is dealing with some kind of challenge and deserves the benefit of the doubt—at least once, anyway. Don't be a jerk.

Acknowledgments

As mentioned in the "Foreword" of this book, I have long wanted to share my experiences and learnings from the Vietnam War and how they did or could apply in business scenarios. Without help and prodding from a number of friends and family, it never would have happened. Lord knows it has taken long enough.

First, my ever-faithful and supportive wife, Helen, has listened to my chatter and always tried to assist with computer questions. She is patient, to say the least.

Without the mentoring and friendship of Dave Weimer, my fellow platoon leader, I would not have benefited from his advice and sense of humor and camaraderie. He was a true leader. Additionally, he connected me with Norm Hinga who led me to Page Publishing and the helpful and competent team there.

My old childhood classmate, Carrie Davis Worthington, was a huge help in transcribing and editing much of my longhand scribbles. She was always a stalwart helper and surprisingly so, considering all the teasing I have given her over our long friendship.

Retired Judge Bill Stewart, who majored in journalism at University of North Carolina at Chapel Hill before going to law school, was a great proofreader and editor. His eye for nuance and resultant input truly helped me clarify and explain many areas.

Steve Stegelin, artist and cartoonist extraordinaire, was able to translate my description of the colonel in the helicopter harassing the lieutenant in the bush just the way I wanted. I love his cover design.

Redcatcher, the 199th Light Infantry Brigade association, and all who served with the unit was also instrumental in providing information about the actions of the unit during the time I served.

Robert J. Gouge's work to chronicle the 199th in several books was also helpful in resurrecting memories. See some of his titles in the suggested reading list. *Raiding the Sanctuary* is particularly revelatory about the Cambodia action.

And of course, I owe much to the young men who served with me in the 199th. They deserve respect and admiration for enduring a very tough and underappreciated assignment those many years ago.

To all, many thanks for bearing with me.

About the Author

William (Dick) D. Rose entered the US Army after dropping out of college in 1968 with the idea of gaining maturity and settling down for a second go at a degree. The experience of combat in Vietnam in 1969 to 1970 proved truly transformative and life-changing. The episodes covered provided confidence and insights, which proved valuable in a successful career of over thirty-five years in the building products industry. His achievements at two industry-leading corporations and an MBA degree were strongly driven by the Vietnam lessons learned. Telling the story and sharing knowledge became a mission, and hopefully, this book will offer both entertaining reading and good advice.